THE HUMAN MACHINE

REPRODUCTION AND GENETICS

Richard Spilsbury

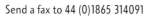

www.heinemann.co.uk/library
Visit our website to find out more information about Heinemann Library books.

To order:
☎ Phone 44 (0)1865 888066
🗏 Send a fax to 44 (0)1865 314091
💻 Visit the Heinemann Bookshop at www.heinemann.co.uk/library to browse our catalogue and order online.

First published in Great Britain by Heinemann,
Halley Court, Jordan Hill, Oxford, OX2 8EJ, part
of Harcourt Education.
Heinemann is a registered trademark of Harcourt
Education Ltd.

Editorial: Nancy Dickmann and Rachel Howells
Design: Victoria Bevan and AMR Design Ltd
Illustrations: Medi-mation
Picture Research: Hannah Taylor
Production: Vicki Fitzgerald

Originated by Chroma
Printed and bound in China by CTPS

ISBN 978 0 431 19205 5 (hardback)
12 11 10 09 08
10 9 8 7 6 5 4 3 2 1

British Library Cataloguing in Publication Data
Spilsbury, Richard, 1963-
Reproduction and genetics. - (The human machine)
1. Human reproduction - Juvenile literature 2.
Human genetics - Juvenile literature 3. Generative
organs - Juvenile literature
I. Title
612.6
A full catalogue record for this book is available
from the British Library.

Acknowledgements
The publishers would like to thank the following
for permission to reproduce photographs: ©Alamy
pp. 25 (Jupiter Images/ Comstock Images), 27
(Zefa RF); ©Corbis pp. 21 (Brand X/ Steve Allen),
4 (Mango Productions), 18 (Rebecca Emery);
©Getty Images pp. 5, 12 (AFP/ Gent Shkullaku),
24 (Ian Waldie), 11 (Rick Gershon), 17 (Riser);
© iStockphoto p. 29 (Justin Horrocks); ©NBAE
via Getty Images p. 19 (Victor Baldizon); Science
Photo Library pp. 10 (Biophoto Associates), 13
(Bluestone), 6 (D. Phillips), 22 (Dr Gopal Murti),
20 (Mauro Fermariello), 14 (Pasieka), 28 (Roger
Harris), 26 (Scott Camazine), 9 (Steve Allen).

Cover photograph of DNA molecule reproduced
with permission of ©Science Photo Library/
Alfred Pasieka.

The publishers would like to thank David Wright
for his assistance in the preparation of this book.

Every effort has been made to contact copyright
holders of any material reproduced in this book.
Any omissions will be rectified in subsequent
printings if notice is given to the publishers.

Contents

Any words appearing in the text in bold, **like this**, are explained in the glossary.

Why do we need to reproduce?

In many ways, the human body is like a machine. Instead of fuel it runs on food, instead of engines it has muscles, and instead of a computer to control it the human body has the brain. Like a machine, a human body eventually wears out. When a machine wears out we buy or make a new one. To make new human machines, people reproduce. They make more living things that look like themselves. If we did not reproduce, there would be no babies born and no children to grow into new adults. Human beings would die out.

LIFE EXPECTANCY

Life expectancy is the average number of years people live. The average lifespan around the world is around 65 for men and 70 for women. These figures are about double what they were 200 years ago because of improvements in healthcare and the quality of food that we eat.

While some machines only last a few years before being worn out, a human being usually lives for 70 years or more from the moment of birth.

All human machines share similar basic features but because of the way we reproduce, there is a lot of variation between individuals.

Why are we all different?

Many machines are made on a production line. Multiple identical copies of the same car or computer roll off conveyor belts every day. They are alike because the parts are exactly the same. Unlike machines made in a factory, each human machine is unique. Humans come in a wide range of shapes and sizes and there is a variety in skin, hair, and eye colour and a million tiny differences in the details of the way we look.

The reason for this variety is the way we reproduce. Many plants reproduce by **asexual reproduction**. This type of reproduction only requires one parent. For example, a part of a plant may break off and grow into a new plant. These new plants will be identical to their single parent. Humans use **sexual reproduction**. This kind of reproduction involves a man and a woman and results in new individuals who are slightly different to each parent.

How do we reproduce?

All living things are made from tiny building blocks called **cells**. The human machine is made up of billions of cells. Sexual reproduction in humans happens when special sex cells, or **gametes**, from different adults combine to create a new individual.

Making gametes

Sperm from men and **eggs** from women are the human gametes. Chromosomes are cross-shaped strands found in the **nucleus**, at the centre of most cells. Chromosomes carry the instructions that tell cells how to function. Most cells have 46 chromosomes, arranged in 23 pairs. Gametes only have 23 chromosomes.

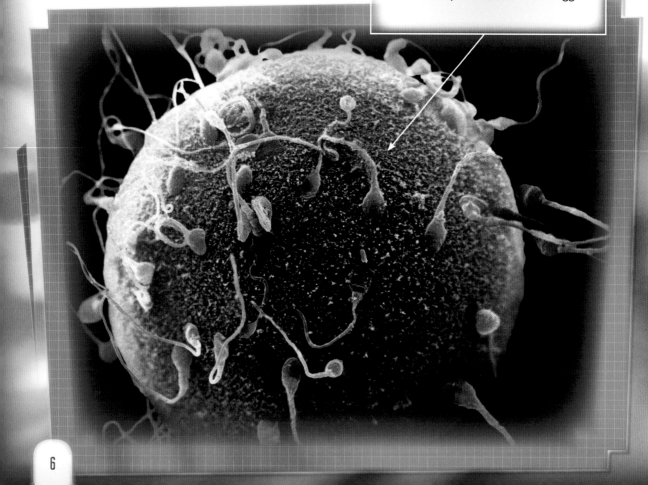

A sperm cell (purple) is a fraction of the size of an egg cell (red). It only takes one sperm to fertilize an egg.

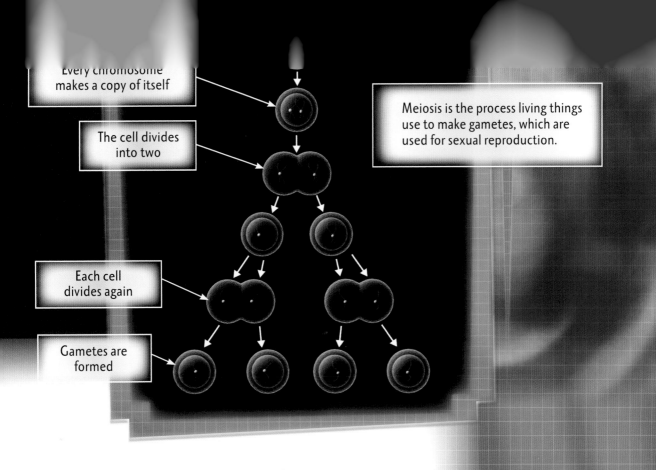

Every chromosome makes a copy of itself

The cell divides into two

Meiosis is the process living things use to make gametes, which are used for sexual reproduction.

Each cell divides again

Gametes are formed

Sex cells form in a process called **meiosis**. Meiosis starts with a cell that has 23 pairs of chromosomes, which is the normal number. Each chromosome makes a copy of itself, creating 46 pairs in the cell. Then the cell divides, or splits, into two, twice. After the first division each cell has 23 pairs of chromosomes. After the second each cell has just 23 chromosomes.

What is fertilization?

A new human is created when a man's sperm joins with an egg inside the woman's body. This is called **fertilization**. During fertilization the 23 chromosomes in the sperm join with the 23 chromosomes in the egg. The chromosomes form pairs. The fertilized egg, or **zygote**, then has 23 pairs of chromosomes just like a normal body cell.

WHERE DOES FERTILIZATION HAPPEN?

The egg and sperm normally fuse inside a woman's body. After fertilization the zygote makes its way to the womb. It stays there for around nine months until the baby is grown and ready to be born.

What happens to the zygote?

The zygote is the start of a new human machine. About 12 hours after fertilization the zygote starts to divide to form two cells. It does this by a process called **mitosis**. Unlike meiosis this process produces cells with the same number of chromosomes in their nuclei as the starting cell.

In mitosis each chromosome pair first copies itself. The pairs line up in the middle of the cell. Then the nucleus splits into two along a line between the pairs. There are then two identical nuclei in one cell. This cell divides between the nuclei making two separate cells. Each of the new cells has exactly the same combination of chromosomes from the mother and the father as the zygote.

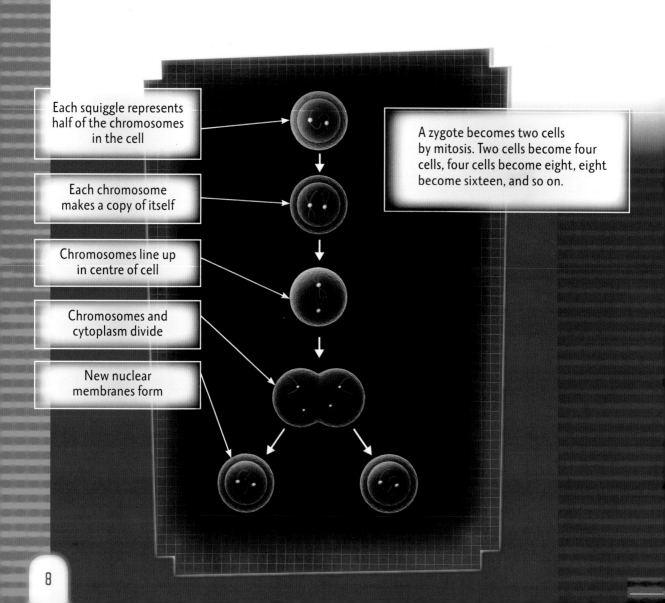

Each squiggle represents half of the chromosomes in the cell

Each chromosome makes a copy of itself

Chromosomes line up in centre of cell

Chromosomes and cytoplasm divide

New nuclear membranes form

A zygote becomes two cells by mitosis. Two cells become four cells, four cells become eight, eight become sixteen, and so on.

Growth and development

The cells of the zygote continue to divide by mitosis about every 12 hours. The increasing number of cells forms a ball. The cells in the ball then start to develop in different ways and take on different shapes. For example, some cells form skin cells, while others form bone or muscle cells. The different cells divide and arrange themselves in the growing baby, making organs such as the brain and heart.

During the first eight weeks after fertilization the growing baby is called an embryo. This embryo is five weeks old. After eight weeks it is called a foetus. That's when we start to see human features such as eyes, fingers, and toes.

RAPID GROWTH

Over nine months, from fertilization to birth, the cells of the new individual greatly increase in number. A zygote is so tiny that five in a row would be the width of a full stop on this page. By the time it is born a baby is made up of millions of cells!

Why do children develop differently?

One of the most obvious differences between babies is their sex – whether they are a boy or a girl. Your sex depends on slight differences in the set of chromosomes you receive at the point of fertilization. The other obvious difference is whether a baby is born on its own or at the same time as one or more brothers or sisters.

Boy or girl?

Most of our cells have 23 pairs of chromosomes. In both males and females 22 of the pairs are identical. However, the 23rd pair is different. This pair decides the sex of an individual. Females have a matching pair of X chromosomes. Males have one X and one Y chromosome.

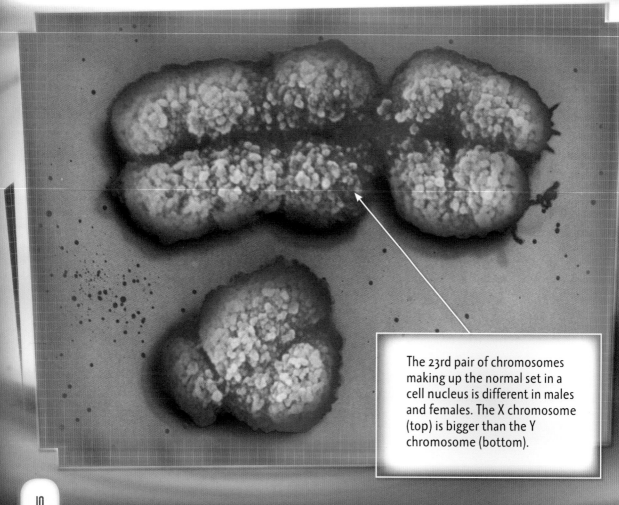

The 23rd pair of chromosomes making up the normal set in a cell nucleus is different in males and females. The X chromosome (top) is bigger than the Y chromosome (bottom).

Identical twins are difficult to tell apart except for small differences, such as fingerprints.

A gamete has just 23 chromosomes. The 23rd chromosome is an X in every egg but either an X or a Y in sperm. It is down to chance whether fertilization produces a boy or a girl. If an X sperm fertilizes an egg, the zygote will have two X chromosomes and develop as a female. If a Y sperm fertilizes an egg, the zygote is male.

Identical twins

Sometimes twins are born that look almost exactly the same. They are called identical twins. Identical twins are produced when the nucleus in a zygote makes a copy of itself before mitosis begins. Then there are two zygotes of the same sex with identical sets of chromosomes. They develop into almost identical babies.

WHAT ARE CONJOINED TWINS?

Once in a while, a zygote only partially divides into identical twins. The twins then develop joined together in some way. They may share some body parts, such as the brain, but develop other parts, such as legs, separately. These twins are called conjoined twins.

Non-identical twins

Only about one in four sets of twins is identical. Most twins are non-identical. They are sometimes called fraternal twins. Non-identical twins develop when two eggs are released and each is fertilized by a different sperm. Two zygotes then start to develop into babies. Most non-identical twins are opposite sex – that is, a boy and a girl. Two girls or two boys is slightly less common. Apart from being almost exactly the same age, non-identical twins are as similar or as different as any other brother and sister, because they have different chromosomes.

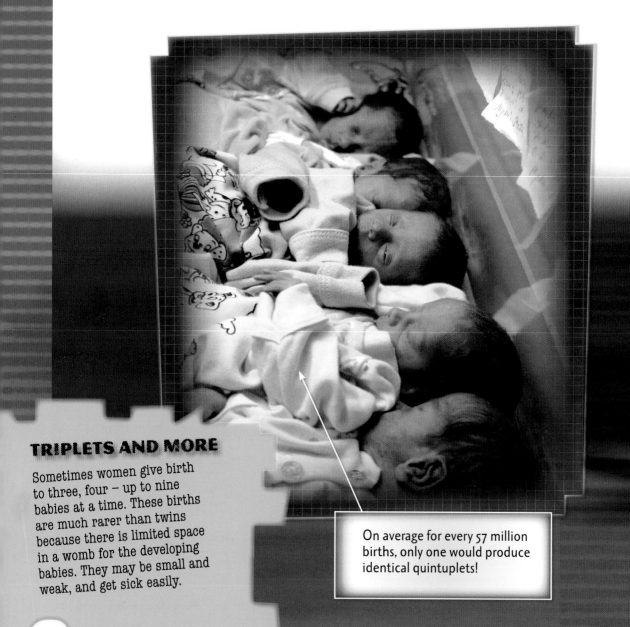

TRIPLETS AND MORE

Sometimes women give birth to three, four – up to nine babies at a time. These births are much rarer than twins because there is limited space in a womb for the developing babies. They may be small and weak, and get sick easily.

On average for every 57 million births, only one would produce identical quintuplets!

Why do children look like their parents?

Think about you and your family. Do the members of your family look alike? Do you have your mum's eyes, or your grandad's nose? Blue eyes or long legs are **inherited traits**. These are characteristics or features passed on from your parents or other ancestors. Inherited traits do not always appear in a straightforward way. They may seem to skip a generation, or affect only the men in a family. The traits are the result of the mixture of chromosomes you have received from your parents and the chromosomes they inherited from your grandparents and earlier generations.

Genes

Genetics is the study of how we inherit traits. Each chromosome is made up of many **genes**, and each gene controls a separate trait. Genes are your body's instruction manual. They spell out, in a chemical code, all the instructions needed to build the human machine. Genes affect not only the way you look, but also some of your abilities, your health, and the way your body works.

Look at the eyes, noses, and mouths of these family members. Can you spot the similarities in traits between generations?

Making the code

Genes are made from a substance called **DNA**. DNA is short for a very complicated sounding name: deoxyribonucleic acid! DNA looks a bit like a ladder twisted into a spiral. Each rung on the DNA ladder is made from a particular sequence of chemicals. Several rungs together make a gene. Imagine that each chemical is represented by a code letter. Groups of the chemicals make up genes rather like letters make up words or sentences. On a single chromosome there are about 50 million letters making up the **genetic code**!

A single chromosome is made of one strand of DNA coiled up. If it was stretched out it would be as much as 8 centimetres (3 inches) long. Coiling allows the strand to take up thousands of times less space than it would if it were stretched. Many chromosomes can then fit easily into the nucleus of a cell.

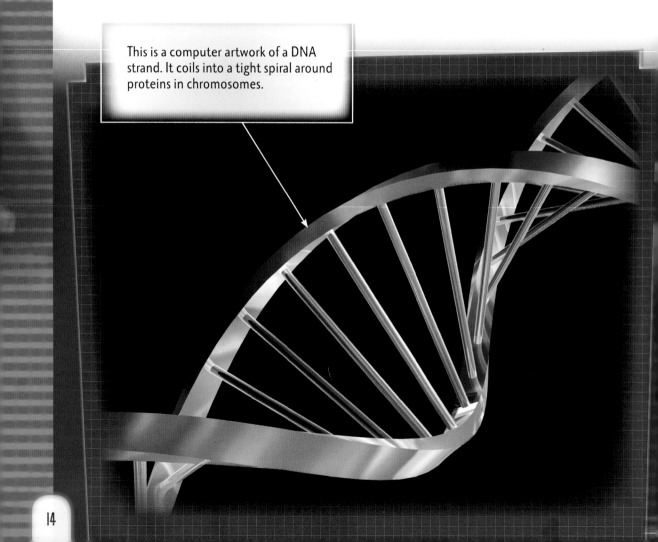

This is a computer artwork of a DNA strand. It coils into a tight spiral around proteins in chromosomes.

Gene identity

Any living thing has a set of genes that is nearly identical to other living things of the same type. This makes it different to other types of living things. So, any human is more like another human than they are, say, to a cat, because the genetic code in their human DNA is different to the genetic code in a cat's DNA. However, the genetic code in each individual human is not exactly the same. Every individual has a unique sequence of chemicals making up their genes.

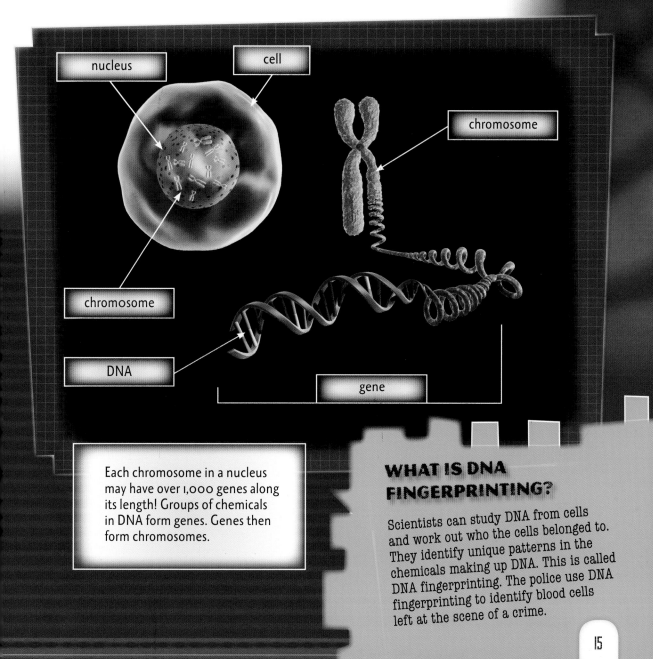

nucleus

cell

chromosome

chromosome

DNA

gene

Each chromosome in a nucleus may have over 1,000 genes along its length! Groups of chemicals in DNA form genes. Genes then form chromosomes.

WHAT IS DNA FINGERPRINTING?

Scientists can study DNA from cells and work out who the cells belonged to. They identify unique patterns in the chemicals making up DNA. This is called DNA fingerprinting. The police use DNA fingerprinting to identify blood cells left at the scene of a crime.

Copying the code

To produce gametes by meiosis, cells must make copies of their genetic code. They do this by unzipping DNA in chromosomes. The DNA ladder breaks halfway through each rung. Then each half combines with other chemicals in the cell to form complete new rungs. There are then two complete DNA strands made of matching sets of genes.

On or off

The total genetic code we inherit is copied exactly during mitosis. This is the way cells increase in number as we grow and develop. It means that nearly every cell in an individual contains the complete genetic code for the whole body. For example, DNA in the muscle cells that form your leg muscles also contains the genes that instruct cells to make eyes a particular colour. However, in any cell only certain genes are active while others are inactive. In a muscle cell only those instructions that tell a muscle how to function are active.

DNA ladder

new strand

This is how DNA unzips and makes copies of itself.

There are lots of knobs on a mixing desk that could change a sound, but only those that are actually turned have an effect. In the human machine, chromosomes contain all the genes for the whole body, but some of them are active and some inactive.

GENE ACTIVITY

The DNA in a single human cell contains about 50,000 genes spread across the 23 pairs of chromosomes. Genes can be inactive in cells in a particular place in the body, but also at particular times of life. For example, genes controlling growing are most active during **puberty**, when your body starts to change from that of a child to that of an adult.

How do genes work?

Builders construct houses using accurate plans drawn by architects. Genes work by supplying the plans needed by cells to repair and make the different parts of your body.

Gene instructions

Cells use the instructions contained in the genetic code to make substances such as **proteins**. These are used to grow and repair the cells making up different body parts such as skin and muscles. They do this by piecing together **nutrients** in the cell. Nutrients are useful substances from food that your body has broken down or digested. It is a bit like the way builders put together bricks, pipes, and other building materials to make a house from a plan.

We may have the same hair colour as our parents because we inherit their genetic code.

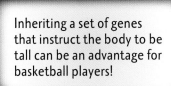
Inheriting a set of genes that instruct the body to be tall can be an advantage for basketball players!

Making traits

Substances that are made using the genetic code create traits. Think of an obvious trait such as your parents' hair and your own. Hair is largely made from protein. Its traits range from curly to straight and from blonde to black. The pairs of hair genes we inherit control our hair trait. If both your parents have genes producing red curly hair, then you will probably inherit those genes and have red curly hair too.

ADDING UP TRAITS

Some traits are determined by the combined effect of more than one pair of genes. For example, how tall you are is determined by the combined size of many bones and other body parts from head to foot. Their growth is controlled by many different genes.

Dominant genes

For each trait you inherit two genes, one from each parent, and they may be different. So, how does your body know which set of instructions to follow? Often one gene for a trait is **dominant**. The instructions it carries are used in preference to those on the other **recessive** gene. For example, in humans the gene instructing our eyes to develop brown irises is dominant. So if a baby inherits a brown eye gene from its mother and a blue eye gene from its father then it will always have brown eyes. Only when both genes are recessive will a recessive trait develop. Therefore, only two blue eye genes will give the recessive blue-eyed trait.

In humans, having brown eyes is the dominant trait and having blue eyes is the recessive trait.

Co-dominance

Sometimes both genes in an inherited pair are equally strong. They are **co-dominant**. An example of this can be found in the four blood groups: A, B, O, and AB. The groups are controlled by three genes—A, B, and O. A and B are co-dominant and O is recessive. You are blood group A if you inherited one A and one O gene, and group B if you inherited one B and one O. But if you inherited one A and one B, you will have blood group AB.

Can you see the number formed by green dots? If you cannot tell you have colour blindness genes.

HOW DO PEOPLE BECOME COLOUR BLIND?

The trait allowing your eyes to distinguish red from green light is dominant. Red-green colour blindness, when you cannot spot the difference, is the recessive trait. The gene for this trait is located only on X chromosomes. Men only have one X chromosome, so they are colour blind if they inherit the recessive gene. Women are only colour blind when both their X chromosomes carry the recessive gene.

What is a Punnett square?

A **Punnett square** is a special grid that is used to predict the possible gene combinations that children could inherit from their parents. It is used to work out how dominant and recessive traits may be passed on between generations. You can make a Punnett square by drawing a grid of four boxes. Write the two possible gene(s) of one parent across the top and the gene(s) of the other down the side. Capital letters represent dominant genes and lower-case letters represent recessive genes. You fill in each box of the Punnett square by transferring the letter above and at the side into them.

Sickle cells are unusually shaped red blood cells that do not last as long or move through the body as well as normal round ones.

sickle cell

normal red blood cell

WHY USE PUNNETT SQUARES?

Many inherited genes are important to our health. Doctors often use Punnett squares to work out the chances of diseases being inherited. For example, sickle cell anaemia is an inherited blood disease. Parents without the disease who have the sickle cell genes may like to know the chances of passing on the disease to their children.

Tongue rolling

Are you a tongue roller? You can do it if you have the dominant (T) gene, which controlled the formation of the right muscles in your tongue. People are not tongue rollers if they have two recessive (t) genes. The Punnett square below represents two parents each with a T and a t gene. The possible gene combinations in their children would be TT, Tt, tT, and tt. Whenever there is T, the child will be a tongue roller. Therefore, there are three tongue rollers to every non-roller.

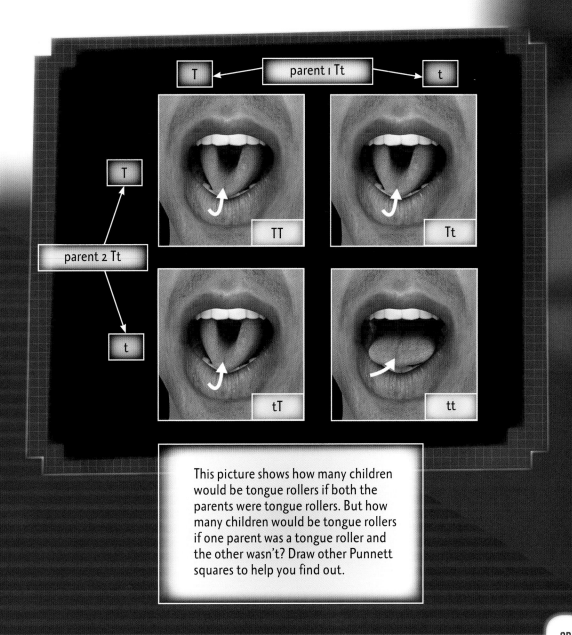

This picture shows how many children would be tongue rollers if both the parents were tongue rollers. But how many children would be tongue rollers if one parent was a tongue roller and the other wasn't? Draw other Punnett squares to help you find out.

Inherited and learned traits

We inherit all sorts of traits from our parents. These range from eye colour and muscle structure to the ability to cry or digest food. All humans inherit genes controlling the development of a brain that can learn and remember information such as what words mean. However, many of your abilities and interests are learned, not inherited. A newborn baby inherits genes for arms and legs, but must be taught to swim. Other learned traits range from knowing how to read to being good at maths.

Athletes may inherit traits such as powerful muscles or long legs that help them do their chosen sport. But they still have to train hard to learn how to do the sport really well.

Environment

People around the world live in different environments, from deserts to coasts and from cities to farms. Your environment is not only the place you live, but also the conditions there and what your life is like. Environment has a big effect on traits. For example, your diet can change how you look. A child with two tall parents may grow up short and weak if the child does not eat the nutrients their body needs to build long, strong bones.

Any trait, such as being able to play a musical instrument, is a mix of what you inherit, what you learn, and the effect of the environment you live in.

HELPFUL INHERITED TRAITS

Inherited traits can make it easier to learn. Musicians may have inherited traits such as good hearing or nimble fingers that help them learn instruments. However, growing up in a musical environment probably had a bigger effect on their learning. Hearing lots of music and watching it being played by parents or friends often makes children keener to learn instruments.

When do people stop growing?

When you are growing, your cells are always dividing into two by mitosis to produce more cells. Some of the most rapid changes to the body happen during puberty, the time when you change from a child to an adult. But how does the body know when to change how fast it grows?

Growing messages

The brain produces chemical messages called growth **hormones** that travel in your blood to the cells. Growth hormones are only made for the first 18 years of a human's life. They tell the cells to divide and increase in number, following the body design set out in your genes, to make you grow to your adult size and appearance. An adult's cells still divide by mitosis, but only to make new cells to replace those that are damaged or become worn out.

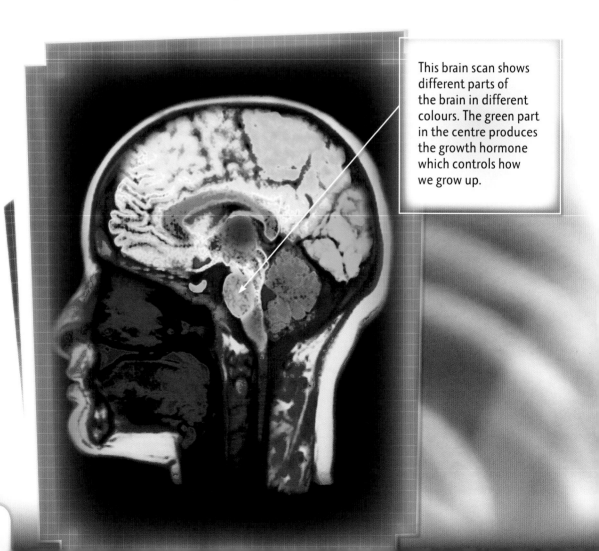

This brain scan shows different parts of the brain in different colours. The green part in the centre produces the growth hormone which controls how we grow up.

When is puberty?

Puberty usually starts when a child is 8 to 10 years old. Puberty hormones instruct you to grow fast into adults. During this time some people grow up to 15 centimetres (6 inches) in one year! The body changes in other ways too. For example, boys and girls usually develop deeper voices and hair grows under their arms. During puberty everyone changes at different rates, so don't worry if you start growing earlier or later than your friends.

Girls are often taller than boys. This is because they start puberty between the ages of 8 and 13, while boys start between 10 and 15. However, many men grow taller than women later in life.

WHICH FOODS HELP ME GROW?

When you are nearing puberty it is especially important to eat a healthy diet, particularly protein-rich and energy-rich foods. Your body needs these to increase the size of your body parts according to the plan set out in your genes.

27

The world's most complex machine

The human body is often described as the world's most complex machine, but of course it is not really a machine at all. Machines are non-living, mechanical objects, whereas our bodies are natural, living things. But there are similarities. Like a machine, the body is made up of different parts that work together in systems to do particular jobs. These different systems work together to make the whole body – or the human machine – run smoothly and efficiently.

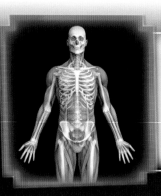

THE SKELETAL SYSTEM

This system of bones supports the other parts of the body, rather as the metal frame of a car supports the vehicle.

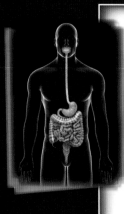

THE DIGESTIVE SYSTEM

The digestive system works as a food-processing machine. It consists of various organs that work together to break down food into forms that the body can use as fuel and raw materials.

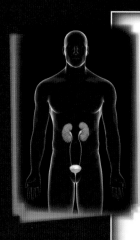

THE EXCRETORY SYSTEM

This is the human machine's waste disposal system, removing harmful substances and waste produced by the other parts of the body.

THE NERVOUS SYSTEM

This is the human machine's communication and control system. The brain transmits and receives messages from the senses and the rest of the body. It does this through a network of nerves connected to the brain via the spinal cord.

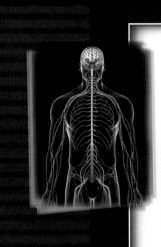

THE CIRCULATORY SYSTEM

This is the body's delivery system. The heart pumps blood through blood vessels, carrying nutrients and oxygen to the other parts and removing waste from cells.

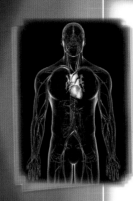

THE RESPIRATORY SYSTEM

This system provides the rest of the body with the oxygen it needs to get energy from food. It also releases waste gases from the body into the air.

THE MUSCULAR SYSTEM

Muscles are the human machine's motors. Some muscles make the bones of the skeleton move; others work as pumps to keep substances moving through the body.

Glossary

asexual reproduction when a living thing creates another identical living thing from part of itself without gametes

cell building block or basic unit of all living things. The human body is made up of millions of different cells.

chromosome strand, found in a nucleus, that carries gene instructions about what the cell does

co-dominant when two genes create traits equally

DNA spiral group of chemicals making up genes on chromosomes

dominant gene that reproduces a trait even if there is only one in a pair

egg female gamete

fertilization when a male gamete joins a female gamete to make a new cell, which grows into a new living thing

gamete sex cell

gene instructions about growth and development found in cells

genetic code sequence of chemicals making up genes on a chromosome

hormone chemical message used by living things to control how and when they develop and grow

inherit receive characteristics of our parents and their ancestors

inherited trait feature developed from genes

meiosis cell division producing gametes different to the starting cell

mitosis process in which cells make exact copies of themselves. Mitosis is vital for the growth and repair of all living things.

nucleus control centre in a cell

nutrient substance that plants and animals need to grow and survive

protein type of nutrient found in foods. Meat is a protein and is vital for the growth and repair of the body.

puberty process that changes a child's body to that of an adult

Punnett square tool people use to predict how genes and traits are inherited

recessive gene that only produces a trait from its instructions when in a pair

sexual reproduction when a living thing creates another living thing that is different to itself by fertilization of gametes

sperm male gamete

trait feature or ability

zygote fertilized egg before cell increase by mitosis occurs

Find out more

Websites

At www.kidshealth.org/kid/talk/qa/what_is_gene.html you can learn more about genes and also different diseases or conditions that can be inherited.

At www.uga.edu/srel/kidsdoscience/games/genetics-code.pdf you can play a game reading the genetic code.

At www.thetech.org/exhibits_events/online/genome/ you can explore how the structure of DNA makes genes and how genes create traits.

Books

Reproduction, Steve Parker (Wayland, 2007)

Reproduction and Growth, Carole Ballard (Franklin Watts, 2005)

Reproduction and Growth, Michaela Miller (KidHaven Press, 2005)

Index